GREAT QUOTES
FROM GREAT
LEADERS

Words *from the* Leaders Who
SHAPED THE WORLD

PEGGY ANDERSON

simple truths
LEAD TO CHANGE

Photo Credits
Cover: front, Wikimedia Commons; White House administration press office
Internals: page 9, Tim Graham /Getty Images; page 10, Bettmann/Getty Images; page 21, Public Domain; page 22, Wikimedia Commons; page 33, Gene Lester/Getty Images; page 34, Alfred Eisenstaedt/Getty Images; page 41, Bettmann/Getty Images; page 42, Wikimedia Commons; page 55, Bettmann/Getty Images; page 56, Library of Congress; page 65, Hulton Archive/Getty Images; page 66, Getty Images/Getty Images; page 77, Time Life Pictures/Getty Images; page 78, Library of Congress; page 89, Hulton Archive/Getty Images; page 90, Fox Photos/Getty Images; page 99, MCT/Getty Images; page 100, Mark Wilson/Getty Images; page 107, MPI/Getty Images; page 108, Library of Congress; page 117, Hulton Archive/Getty Images; page 118, Fine Art/Getty Images; page 127, Wikimedia Commons; page 128, Mara Vivat/Getty Images; page 135, Evening Standard/Getty Images; page 136, Hank Walker/Getty Images; page 145, AFP/Getty Images; page 146, Hulton Archive/Getty Images; page 157, Bettmann/Getty Images; page 158, Art Shay/Getty Images; page 163, Library of Congress; page 164, Alexander Gardner/Getty Images; page 175, NY Daily News; page 176, Vince Lombardi Jr.; page 185, Historical/Getty Images; page 186, Fotosearch/Getty Images; Page 191, Walter Dhladhla; page 192, Wikimedia Commons; page 203, Wikimedia Commons; page 204, Bettmann/Getty Images; page 213, Wikimedia Commons; page 214, White House Administration Press Office; page 225, Time Life Pictures/Getty Images; page 226, Margaret Bourke-White/Getty Images; page 233, Jerome Delay/Getty Images; page 234, Harry Langdon/Getty Images; page 245, Thomas D. McAvoy/Getty Images; page 246, Hulton Archive/Getty Images; page 255, American Stock Archive/Getty Images; page 256, Wikimedia Commons; page 267, MPI /Getty Images; page 268, Library of Congress; page 281, Hulton Archive/Getty Images; page 282, Bettmann/Getty Images; page 293, Terry O'Neill/Getty Images; page 294, Keystone /Getty Images; page 301, Eliot Elisofon/Getty Images; page 302, Library of Congress; page 309, Public Domain; page 310, Bettmann/Getty Images; page 317, Public Domain; page 318, Library of Congress ; page 327, ullstein bild /Getty Images; page 328, Three Lions/Getty Images; page 337, Bettmann/Getty Images; page 338, Wikimedia Commons; page 345, Gerard Julien/Getty Images; page 346, Public Domain

Published by Simple Truths, an imprint of Sourcebooks, Inc.
P.O. Box 4410, Naperville, Illinois 60567–4410
(630) 961-3900
Fax: (630) 961-2168
www.sourcebooks.com

Printed and bound in China.

QL 10 9 8 7 6 5 4 3 2 1

Dedicated with love and
gratitude to my mother Mary
and my stepfather Richard Crisorio.

CONTENTS

INTRODUCTION

Throughout history, the words of great leaders have inspired, comforted, persuaded, and motivated.

Regardless of their fields of endeavor, they were all visionaries who led by example and whose actions transformed ideas into constructive form.

This collection of timeless wisdom echoes the integrity, strength of character, and passion of these extraordinary men and women.

I hope that you will enjoy this book and use it as a source of knowledge and inspiration.

Peggy Anderson

"

We ourselves feel that what we are doing is just a drop in the ocean. But if that drop was not in the ocean, I think the ocean would be less because of that missing drop.

"

MOTHER
TERESA

Mother Teresa, born Agnes Gonxha Bojaxhiu, is revered for her lifelong dedication to the poor, most notably the destitute masses of India.

In 1928, at the age of eighteen, she went to Ireland to join the Loreto Convent in Rathfarnam, Dublin, and shortly thereafter traveled to India to work

with the poor of Calcutta. In 1950, after studying nursing, she moved into the slums of the city and founded the Order of the Missionaries of Charity. Mother Teresa was summoned to Rome in 1968 to found a home for the needy, and three years later, she was awarded the first Pope John

XXIII Peace Prize. By the late 1970s, the Missionaries of Charity numbered more than a thousand nuns who operated sixty centers in Calcutta and over two hundred centers worldwide.

Mother Teresa's selfless commitment to helping the poor saved the lives of nearly 8,000 people in Calcutta alone. Her compassion and devotion to the destitute earned her the Nobel Peace Prize in 1979. Following her death, Mother Teresa was beatified by Pope John Paul II.

The **hunger for love** is much more difficult to remove than the hunger for bread.

▼

Don't look for big things, just do small things with **great love.**

I see GOD in every
human being. When I
wash the leper's wounds
I feel I am nursing
the Lord himself.

We can never know how much
good a **simple smile** can do.

▼

Loneliness and the feeling of being
unwanted is the most terrible poverty.

▼

Now let us do something
beautiful for **God.**

Do not allow yourself to be disheartened by any failure **as long as you have done your best.**

▼

It is very important for us to realize that love, to be true, has to hurt. I must be willing to give whatever it takes not to harm other people and, in fact, to do good to them.

A joyful heart is the **inevitable result**

of a heart burning with love.

Bring love into your home, for this is where

our love for each other must start.

If I ever become a Saint—I will surely be one of "darkness." I will continually be absent from HEAVEN—to light the light of those in darkness on earth.

Humility is the mother of all virtues;
purity, charity, and obedience.

▼

If anyone wants to help me, let them
begin at home. There is help needed
on your doorstep, in your place of work,
in your office, and in your factory.

Instead of death and sorrow, let us bring **peace** and **joy** to the world.

▼

Love is a fruit in season at all times, and within reach of every hand.

▼

Let no one ever come to you without leaving **better** and **happier.**

"

I have nothing to offer but blood, toil, tears, and sweat.

"

WINSTON
CHURCHILL

Sir Winston Churchill—author, orator, and statesman—led Great Britain from the brink of defeat to victory as wartime prime minister. Born in Oxfordshire, England, in 1874, Churchill began serving his country as a military leader in the Boer War and later as a prominent leader during World War I. As a member

of Parliament, his repeated warnings of the menace of Hitler's Germany, combined with his aggressive and convincing oratory skills, resulted in his appointment to prime minister in 1940.

He joined Franklin D. Roosevelt and Joseph Stalin in

1940 to shape Allied strategy in World War II. An intense patriot and a romantic believer in his country's greatness, Churchill gave his people the strong leadership and devotion that ultimately led to Britain's military salvation.

He was awarded the Nobel Prize for literature in 1953, largely due to his book *The Second World War*, and was also knighted the same year.

The empires of the **future** are

the empires of the **mind.**

▼

Courage is going from failure to

failure without losing enthusiasm.

If we are together NOTHING is impossible. If we are divided all will fail.

No one can guarantee success
in war, but only deserve it.

▼

Never give in—never, never, never,
never, in nothing great or small, large
or petty, never give in except to
convictions of honor and good sense.

All the greatest things are **simple,** and many can be expressed in a single word: freedom, justice, honor, duty, mercy, hope.

The price of greatness is **responsibility.**

Every day you may make progress. Every step may be fruitful. Yet there will stretch out before you an ever-lengthening, ever-ascending, ever-improving path. You know you will never get to the end of the journey. But this, so far from discouraging, only **adds to the joy and glory of the climb.**

Give us the tools, and we will finish the job.

It is a mistake to look too far ahead. Only one link in the chain of destiny can be handled at a time.

▼

To build may have to be the slow and laborious task of **years.** To destroy can be the thoughtless act of a **single day.**

Difficulties **mastered** are opportunities **won.**

▼

It's not enough that we do our best;

sometimes we have to do what's required.

▼

I never worry about action, but only inaction.

Courage is rightly
esteemed the first of
human QUALITIES,
because, as has been
said, "It is the quality
which guarantees
all others."

"
Fancy being
remembered
around the world
for the invention
of a mouse!
"

WALT
DISNEY

Walt Disney, the pioneer of animated cartoon films, displayed his creative talents at an early age. His interest in art led him to study cartooning through a correspondence school, and he later took classes at the Kansas City Art Institute and School of Design.

In the late 1920s, Disney recognized the potential for sound in cartoon films. He produced *Steamboat Willie*, a cartoon short equipped with voices and music, and the character of Mickey Mouse was introduced to the public.

WALT DISNEY

During the economic hard times of the 1930s, Disney's cartoons captivated his audiences. His body of work firmly established him as the unparalleled master of feature-length animated films.

Walt Disney received twenty-two Academy Awards and four Emmy nominations, winning one of them. His creativity, ingenuity, and ability to bring his fantasies to fruition continue to enchant all ages.

I only hope that we never lose sight of one thing—that it was **all started by a mouse.**

▼

You may not realize it when it happens, but a kick in the teeth may be the best thing in the world for you.

▼

When you believe in a thing, **believe in it all the way,** implicitly and unquestionably.

The way to get started is to quit talking and begin doing.

▼

Our greatest natural resource is the **minds** of our children.

Our heritage and ideals, our codes and standards—the things we live by and teach our children—are **preserved or diminished** by how freely we exchange ideas and feelings.

▼

It's kind of fun to do the impossible.

We keep moving forward, opening up new doors and doing new things, because we're curious and curiosity keeps leading us down new paths.

▼

Disneyland will never be completed. It will continue to grow as long as there is **imagination** left in the world.

"

Imagination is more important than knowledge.

"

ALBERT
EINSTEIN

ALBERT EINSTEIN

One of the greatest scientific minds of all time, Albert Einstein is best known for his contributions to the field of physics. Born in Germany in 1879, Einstein received his diploma from the Swiss Federal Polytechnic School in Zurich, where he trained as a teacher in physics and mathematics. In 1905, he received his PhD and published four research papers, the most significant being the creation of the special theory of relativity. He became internationally famous when he was awarded the Nobel Prize for Physics in 1921.

ALBERT EINSTEIN

The important military implications of the discovery of the fission of uranium in 1939 led Einstein to appeal to President Franklin Roosevelt. Einstein's letter to the president led to the development of the atomic bomb.

Einstein left the field of physics greatly changed through his brilliant contributions. His discoveries provided the impetus for future research into understanding the mysteries of the universe.

The ideals that have LIGHTED my way, and time after time have given me new courage to face life cheerfully, have been kindness, beauty, and truth.

The important thing is not to stop questioning. **Curiosity has its own reason for existence.** One cannot help but be in awe when he contemplates the mysteries of eternity, of life, of the marvelous structure of reality. It is enough if one tries merely to comprehend a little of this mystery each day. Never lose a holy curiosity.

Truth is what stands the test of experience.

▼

Try to become not a man of success, but try rather to become a man of **value.**

▼

God is subtle, but He is not malicious.

The most important human endeavor is the **striving** for morality in our **action.** Our inner balance and even our very existence depend on it. Only **morality** in our actions can give beauty and dignity to life.

When I examined myself, and my methods of thought, I came to the conclusion that the gift of FANTASY has meant more to me than my talent for absorbing positive knowledge.

Weakness of attitude becomes
weakness of character.

▼

Whoever is **careless with truth**
in small matters cannot be
trusted in important affairs.

A person who never made a mistake never tried anything **new.**

Science without religion is lame, religion without science is blind.

Common sense is nothing more than a deposit of prejudices laid down in the mind before you reach eighteen.

The distinction between past, present, and future is only an ILLUSION, however persistent.

Intellectuals solve problems, GENIUSES prevent them.

I never think of the future. It comes soon enough.

▼

The eternal mystery of the world is its comprehensibility… The fact that it is **comprehensible** is a **miracle.**

"

A people that values its privileges above its principles soon loses both.

DWIGHT D.
EISENHOWER

It was a blend of honesty, humility, and persistence that marked Dwight D. Eisenhower's success as both the thirty-fourth president of the United States and as the supreme commander of the Allied forces during World War II.

Eisenhower graduated from West Point and commanded a tank training center during World War

I. At the outbreak of World War II, Eisenhower was appointed to the army's war plans division, where he prepared strategy for the Allied invasion of Europe. He was later selected commander of U.S. troops in Europe.

He retired from the military to become president of Columbia

University and publish his bestselling account of the war. Wooed by both parties, Eisenhower ran as a Republican for president in 1952 and 1956, winning both times. Eisenhower enjoyed tremendous popularity with the American people and worked to expand Social Security and increase the minimum wage. In addition, he created the Departments of Health, Education, and Welfare, and NASA.

The final battle against intolerance is to be fought—not in the chambers of any legislature—but in the HEARTS of men.

The supreme quality for leadership is **unquestionably integrity.** Without it, no real success is possible.

When you are in any contest, you should work as if there were, to the very last minute, a chance to lose it.

Only **strength** can cooperate.
Weakness can only beg.

Pessimism never won any battle.

Only our individual faith in
freedom can keep us free.

You don't lead by hitting people over the head—that's assault, not leadership.

▼

A **sense of humor** is part of the art of leadership, of getting along with people, of getting things done.

May we grow in **strength**—without pride of self. May we, in our dealings with all peoples of the earth, ever **speak truth** and serve justice… May the light of **freedom,** coming to all darkened lands, flame brightly— until at last the darkness is no more.

DWIGHT D. EISENHOWER

The history of free men
is never really written
by chance but by
CHOICE—their choice.

Anybody can do anything that he imagines.

HENRY
FORD

Celebrated as both a technological genius and a folk hero, Henry Ford was the creative force in the automotive industry. His innovations changed the economic and social character of his country—and the world.

Ford developed the mass-produced Model T automobile and sold it at a price the average person could afford. Use of the assembly line in mass production saved time and money and allowed Ford to offer more cars to the American public at a lower price than anyone before him. More than fifteen million Model Ts were sold in the United States between 1908 and 1927.

A noted philanthropist, Ford established Greenfield Village, a group of historical buildings and landmarks in Dearborn, Michigan. He also established the Henry Ford Museum and the Ford Foundation.

Quality means **doing it right** when no one is looking.

▼

A business that makes nothing but money is a poor kind of business.

History is more or less bunk. It's tradition. We don't want tradition. We want to live in the present, and the only history that is worth a tinker's dam is the history we MAKE today.

An **idealist** is a person who helps other people to be **prosperous.**

▼

Change is not always progress… A fever of newness has been everywhere confused with the spirit of progress.

Before everything else, **getting ready** is the secret of success.

▼

What we call evil is simply ignorance bumping its head in the dark.

▼

If everyone is moving forward **together,** then success takes care of itself.

I cannot discover that anyone knows enough to say definitely what is and what is not POSSIBLE.

Most people spend more time and energy going around problems than trying to solve them.

▼

Wealth, like happiness, is **never attained** when sought after directly. It comes as a **byproduct** of providing a useful service.

The whole secret of a **successful life** is to find out what it is one's **destiny** to do, and then do it.

▼

You can't build a reputation on what you're going to do.

Life is a series of experiences, each of which makes us bigger, even though it is hard to realize this. **For the world was built to develop character,** and we must learn that the setbacks and griefs which we endure help us in our marching onward.

"

If you desire many
things, many things
will seem but a few.

BENJAMIN
FRANKLIN

American printer, publisher, author, inventor, scientist, and diplomat, Benjamin Franklin is best remembered for his role in separating the American colonies from Great Britain and in helping to frame the Declaration of Independence.

Franklin continued his efforts as an inventor and scientist throughout his diplomatic career, inventing the Franklin stove, bifocal spectacles, and the lightning rod. He was the first to institute such public services as a fire department, a lending library, and a learning academy, which later became the University of Pennsylvania.

He served as a delegate to the Second Continental Congress and then traveled to France to seek military and financial aid for the warring colonies. Franklin was also one of the diplomats chosen to negotiate peace with Britain at the war's end and was instrumental in achieving the adoption of the U.S. Constitution.

Lost time is never found again.

▼

The doors of **wisdom** are never shut.

▼

A house is not a home unless it contains food and fire for the mind as well as the body.

There never was a good war, or a bad peace.

As we must account for every idle word, so must we account for every idle silence.

All mankind is divided into three classes: those that are **immovable,** those that are **movable,** and those that **move.**

In this world, nothing can be said to be certain, except death and taxes.

At twenty years of age, the will reigns; at thirty the wit; and at forty, the judgment.

He that lives upon **hope** will die fasting.

Be slow in choosing a friend, slower in changing.

Half a truth is often a **great lie.**

▼

He does not possess wealth;

it possesses him.

▼

The discontented man finds no **easy chair.**

Life's TRAGEDY is that we get old too soon and wise too late.

Remember that time is money.

Well done is better than well said.

Words may show a man's wit

but **actions** his meaning.

Take TIME for all things: great haste makes great waste.

" "

Happiness is when what you think, what you say, and what you do are in harmony.

" "

MAHATMA
GANDHI

MAHATMA GANDHI

Leader of the Indian Nationalist movement against British rule, Mohandas "Mahatma" Gandhi is revered as the father of his country. He is esteemed internationally for his doctrine of nonviolence to achieve political and social progress.

Gandhi received an education in India before

beginning law studies in England in 1888. Seeking clerical work in South Africa, he was shocked at the racial discrimination he encountered. He became an advocate for his fellow Indians, and his challenges to the government resulted in a jail sentence.

MAHATMA GANDHI

He entered politics in India in 1919 to protest British sedition laws. He emerged as the head of the Indian National Congress, where he advocated a policy of nonviolent protest to achieve Indian independence. Repressed throughout World War II, Gandhi successfully negotiated for an autonomous Indian state in 1947. He was assassinated one year later.

A coward is incapable
of exhibiting love;
it is the prerogative
of the BRAVE.

Nonviolence is not a garment to be put on and off at will. Its seat is in the **heart,** and it must be an inseparable part of our being.

"

In my humble opinion, noncooperation with evil is as much a duty as is cooperation with GOOD.

A man is but the product of his thoughts.
What he thinks, he becomes.

Nonviolence is the first article of my **faith.**
It is also the last article of my **creed.**

Glory lies in the attempt to reach
one's goal and not in reaching it.

MAHATMA GANDHI

Power is of two kinds. One is obtained by the fear of punishment and the other by acts of love. Power based on love is a thousand times more effective and permanent than the one derived from fear of punishment.

▼

An ounce of **practice** is worth more than tons of **preaching.**

The moment a slave resolves that he will no longer be a slave, his fetters fall. He frees himself and shows the way to others. **Freedom and slavery are mental states.**

Love never claims, it ever gives. Love ever suffers, never resents, never revenges itself.

"The side that wants to take the choice away from women and give it to the state, they're fighting a losing battle. Time is on the side of change.

RUTH
BADER GINSBURG

Ruth Bader Ginsburg is an Associate Justice of the Supreme Court of the United States, which makes her the second female justice in the country's history. Encouraged by her mother to embrace education, Ginsburg enrolled at Harvard Law School as one of nine females in a class size of approximately 500 students. She transferred to Columbia Law School after her husband took a job in New York City, becoming the first woman to be on two major law reviews—the *Columbia Law Review* and the *Harvard Law Review*.

Ginsburg's start to her legal career was not ideal; being a mother to a young child, a wife, and Jewish at a dangerous time in our history, she struggled to find a job. Eventually, Ginsburg became an associate director of the Columbia Law School Project on International Procedure and spent time in Sweden where she began to develop more insight on gender equality. Back in the States, Ginsburg became a professor at Rutgers Law School and was one of less than twenty female professors in the country.

Ginsburg has devoted most of her career to fighting for women's rights as a constitutional principle. In 1972, she cofounded the Women's Rights Project at the American Civil Liberties Union and between 1973 and 1976, she argued six gender discrimination cases before the Supreme Court and won five of them. In 2009, *Forbes* named her among the 100 Most Powerful Women.

RUTH BADER GINSBURG

People ask me
sometimes, "When will
there be enough women
on the court?" And
my answer is: "WHEN
THERE ARE NINE."

RUTH BADER GINSBURG

We should not be held back from **pursuing our full talents,** from contributing what we could **contribute to the society,** because we fit into a certain mold—because we belong to a group that historically has been the object of discrimination.

If you have a caring life partner, you **help the other person when that person needs it.** I had a life partner who thought my work was as important as his, and I think that made all the difference for me.

Every now and then it HELPS to be a LITTLE DEAF... That advice has stood me in good stead. Not simply in dealing with my marriage, but in dealing with my colleagues.

**Desperate courage
makes one a
majority.**

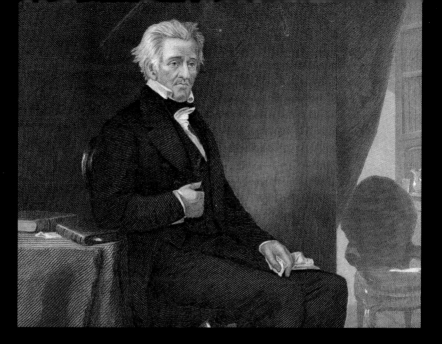

ANDREW
JACKSON

ANDREW JACKSON

Born in a log cabin in the wilds of the Carolinas and orphaned at the age of fourteen, Andrew Jackson grew up with the frontier spirit of one always ready to defend and honor his country. His self-reliance and determination would serve him well as a lawyer, judge, congressman, senator, military hero, and the seventh president of the United States.

It was his heroism in the War of 1812 that earned him the nickname "Old Hickory" and thrust him into national prominence. Jackson and his Tennessee militia defeated the British at New Orleans, marking the end of the fighting.

His military triumphs led to his nomination as president, and he was elected in 1828. His election marked the first time a president was elected from the area west of the Appalachians and the first time an election focused on direct mass appeal to the voters. This rising tide of democratic sentiment became known as "Jacksonian democracy."

As long as our **government** is administered for the good of the people, and is regulated by their will; as long as it secures to us the rights of persons and of property, liberty of conscience, and of the press, it will be worth **defending.**

The BRAVE man inattentive to his duty, is worth little more to his country than the coward who deserts her in the hour of danger.

I have accustomed myself to receive with respect the opinions of others but always take the RESPONSIBILITY of deciding for myself.

Every good citizen makes his country's **honor** his own, and cherishes it not only as precious but as **sacred.** He is willing to risk his life in its defense and is conscious that he gains protection while he gives it.

▼

You are uneasy; you've never sailed with **me** before, I see.

PEACE, above all things, is to be desired, but blood must sometimes be spilled to obtain it on equable and lasting terms.

You must pay the price if you wish

to **secure the blessing.**

▼

Take time to deliberate; but when the time

for action arrives, stop thinking and go in.

"

The boisterous sea
of liberty is never
without a wave.

THOMAS
JEFFERSON

THOMAS JEFFERSON

The third president of the United States and its first secretary of state, Thomas Jefferson is best remembered as the principal author of the Declaration of Independence.

A wealthy Virginia planter, Jefferson began his political career as a member of the House of Burgesses

in 1769. Later, as a delegate to the Second Continental Congress, he was appointed along with Benjamin Franklin and John Adams to draft a formal statement of reasons for separation from Great Britain. The resultant Declaration of Independence, largely penned by Jefferson, summed up the commitment of the young country to life, liberty, and self-government.

He went on to serve as the U.S. minister in France before accepting George Washington's appointment as the first secretary of state. Assuming the presidency in 1801, he soon doubled the size of the United States with the purchase of the Louisiana Territory from Napoleon. He devoted his life in retirement to establishing the University of Virginia.

The **will of the people** is the only legitimate foundation of any government, and to protect its free expression should be our first object.

▼

Determine never to be idle… It is **wonderful** how much may be done if we are always doing.

Delay is preferable to **error.**

It is neither wealth nor splendor,

but tranquility and occupation

which give happiness.

An honest man can feel **no pleasure** in the exercise of power over his fellow citizens.

▼

We hold these truths to be self-evident: That all men are created equal; that they are endowed by their Creator with certain unalienable rights; that among these are life, liberty, and the pursuit of happiness.

A coward is much more exposed to quarrels than a man of spirit.

▼

For here we are not afraid to follow **truth** wherever it may lead.

That government is the **strongest** of which every man feels himself a part.

There is not a truth existing which I fear or would wish unknown to the whole world.

Whenever you do a thing, act as if all the WORLD were watching.

"
The bulk of the
world's knowledge
is an imaginary
construction.
"

HELEN
KELLER

Helen Adams Keller was born in Tuscumbia, Alabama, in 1880. A severe illness in infancy left her deprived of sight, hearing, and the ability to speak. Her life represents one of the most extraordinary examples of a person who was able to transcend her physical handicaps—accomplishing more with her impairments than many do in their lifetimes.

Through the constant and patient instruction of Anne Sullivan, Helen Keller not only learned to read, write, and speak but went on to graduate cum laude from Radcliffe College in 1904. In addition to writing several articles, books, and biographies and cofounding the American Civil Liberties Union, she was active on the staffs of the American Foundation for the Blind and the American Foundation for the Overseas Blind. She also lectured in over twenty-five countries and received several awards of great distinction.

Helen Keller's courage, faith, and optimism in the face of such overwhelming disabilities had a profound effect on all she touched. Her tremendous accomplishments stand as a symbol of human potential.

Alone we can
do so little; TOGETHER
we can do so much.

Security is mostly a superstition. It does not exist in nature, nor do the children of men as a whole experience it. Avoiding danger is no safer in the long run than outright exposure. **Life is either a daring adventure or nothing.**

▼

Keep your face to the sunshine and you cannot see the shadows.

The Bible gives me a deep, comforting sense that "things seen are temporal, and things unseen are ETERNAL."

Happiness cannot come from without. It must come from within. It is not what we see and touch or that which others do for us which makes us happy; it is that which we **think and feel and do, first for the other fellow** and then for ourselves.

We need men
who can dream
of things that
never were, and
ask why not.

JOHN F.
KENNEDY

JOHN F. KENNEDY

John F. Kennedy was elected the thirty-fifth president of the United States at the age of forty-three—the youngest man and first Roman Catholic ever elected.

Kennedy graduated from Harvard University in 1940 and joined the U.S. Navy shortly before World War II. While on active duty in the Pacific, the Japanese destroyed the boat under his command, *PT-109*. Despite a back injury, Kennedy showed great heroism in rescuing his crew.

After holding seats in both the House and Senate, Kennedy was elected president in 1960. His style, charisma, and oratory won him admiration at home and abroad, but his life was tragically cut short by an assassin's bullet in 1963. His major accomplishments include the formation of the Peace Corps and his deft handling of the Cuban Missile Crisis. His book, *Profiles in Courage*, won the Pulitzer Prize in 1957.

The American, by nature, is optimistic. He is experimental, an inventor and a builder who BUILDS best when called upon to build greatly.

JOHN F. KENNEDY

We stand for **freedom.** That is our conviction for ourselves—that is our only commitment to others.

In a free society **art is not a weapon...** Artists are not engineers of the soul.

My fellow Americans, ask not what your country can do for you, ask what you can do for YOUR country.

There are risks and costs to a program of **action.** But they are far less than the long-range risks and costs of comfortable **inaction.**

We stand today on the edge of a **new frontier.**

Liberty without learning is always in **peril;** learning without liberty is always in **vain.**

Mankind must put an end to war— or war will put an end to mankind.

There's an old saying that victory has a hundred fathers and defeat is an orphan.

▼

Change is the law of life. Those who look only to the past or the present are certain to miss the future.

"

The time is
always right to do
what is right.

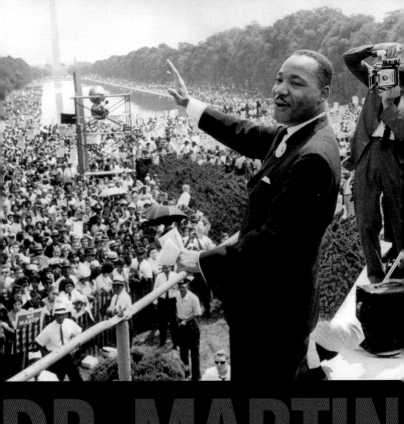

DR. MARTIN
LUTHER KING JR.

Martin Luther King Jr. used his strong personality and eloquent oratory to spearhead the civil rights movement in the United States during the 1950s and 1960s. A Baptist minister, King began his civil rights activities in 1955 with the successful boycott of the segregated bus system in Montgomery, Alabama.

The Southern Christian Leadership Conference was founded in 1957 in an effort to mobilize the nonviolent struggle against racism and discrimination; King was named its first president. On August 28, 1963, the massive March on Washington culminated in

250,000 Americans of all races gathering at the Lincoln Memorial to hear King speak.

The movement won a major victory in 1964, when Congress passed the Civil Rights Act, and King became the youngest man ever to receive the Nobel Peace Prize. The world lost a towering symbol of liberty and justice when an assassin's bullet claimed his life in 1968.

Human progress is neither automatic nor inevitable… **Every step toward the goal of justice requires sacrifice, suffering, and struggle;** the tireless exertions and passionate concern of dedicated individuals.

And it may well be that we will have to repent in this generation. Not merely for the vitriolic words and the violent actions of the bad people, but for the appalling silence and indifference of the GOOD people.

I have a **dream** that one day this nation will rise up and live out the true meaning of its creed: "We hold these truths to be self-evident: **that all men are created equal.**"

▼

It is not possible to be in favor of justice for some people and not be in favor of justice for all people.

The ultimate measure of a man is not where he stands in moments of comfort and convenience, but where he stands at times of **challenge and controversy.**

Injustice **anywhere** is a threat to justice **everywhere.**

Love is the only force capable of transforming an **enemy** into a friend.

If a man has not discovered something that he will die for, he isn't fit to live.

The **quality,** not the longevity, of one's life is what is **important.**

Wars are poor chisels for carving out **peaceful** tomorrows.

▼

Every person must decide at some point whether they will walk in the **light** of creative altruism or in the **darkness** of destructive selfishness. This is the judgment. Life's most persistent and urgent question is, **"What are you doing for others?"**

DR. MARTIN LUTHER KING JR.

We must either learn to live together
as brothers or we are all going
to perish together as fools.

A man-made code that squares with the
moral law, or the **law of God,** is a just law.

Now is the time to make justice a
reality for all of God's children.

I believe that unarmed truth and unconditional love will have the FINAL word in reality.

"

Luck is a dividend of sweat–the more you sweat, the luckier you get.

RAY KROC

RAY KROC

As founder of the McDonald's Corporation, Ray A. Kroc is largely responsible for revolutionizing the restaurant industry. His persistence, diligence, and faithfulness set the standard for modern business leadership.

Kroc's opportunity for success came in the form of a small restaurant in San Bernardino, California,

run by the McDonald brothers. Their assembly-line method of serving hamburgers, french fries, and shakes was simple but efficient. Kroc knew that this concept would have a great appeal to consumers.

Kroc opened his first McDonald's on April 15, 1955.

Kroc continued to expand by introducing a unique franchise system. His methods and ideas about customer service have served as models for many different industries.

Kroc's steadfast devotion to an idea brought him personal success and also allowed him to set up several charities and educational organizations.

RAY KROC

Are you green and GROWING or ripe and rotting?

RAY KROC

"

If you work just for money, you'll never make it, but if you **love what you're doing** and you always **put the customer first,** success will be yours.

"

I claim not to have controlled events, but confess plainly that events have controlled me.

ABRAHAM
LINCOLN

ABRAHAM LINCOLN

The sixteenth president of the United States, Abraham Lincoln preserved the Union during the American Civil War. Lincoln's inner qualities of faithfulness, honesty, resolution, humor, and courage gave him the strength to lead his country during the bloodiest years of its existence.

Born in the backwoods of Kentucky in 1809, Lincoln worked as a rail splitter, flatboatman, storekeeper, postmaster, and surveyor before becoming a lawyer. His debates while running for the Senate made him a nationally known figure, and he was elected president in 1860.

By the time Lincoln had taken office, seven states had already seceded from the Union over the issue of slavery. Lincoln issued his Emancipation Proclamation in 1863 to set the slaves in the rebellious states free. Reelected in 1864, Lincoln was tragically assassinated before he could oversee the Reconstruction of the South.

Those who deny FREEDOM to others, deserve it not for themselves; and, under a just God, cannot long retain it.

I leave you, hoping that the **lamp of liberty** will burn in your bosoms until there shall no longer be a doubt that all men are created free and equal.

▼

Let us have faith that right makes might, and in that faith, let us, to the end, dare to do our duty as we understand it.

Four score and seven years ago our Fathers brought forth on this continent a new nation, conceived in **liberty and dedicated** to the proposition that all men are created equal.

▼

Force is all-conquering, but its **victories** are short-lived.

Stand with anybody that stands right. Stand with him while he is RIGHT and part with him when he goes wrong.

The **probability** that we may fall in the struggle **ought not** to deter us from the support of a cause we believe to be just.

▼

"A house divided against itself cannot stand." I believe this government cannot endure, permanently half slave and half free.

I am rather inclined to SILENCE, and whether that be wise or not, it is at least more unusual nowadays to find a man who can hold his tongue than to find one who cannot.

The man does not live who is more devoted to PEACE than I am, none who would do more to preserve it.

ABRAHAM LINCOLN

As I would not be a slave, so I would not be a master. **This expresses my idea of democracy.** Whatever differs from this, to the extent of the difference, is no democracy.

▼

I do not think much of a man who is not wiser today than he was yesterday.

> **Winning is not a sometime thing... You don't do things right once in a while; you do them right all of the time.**

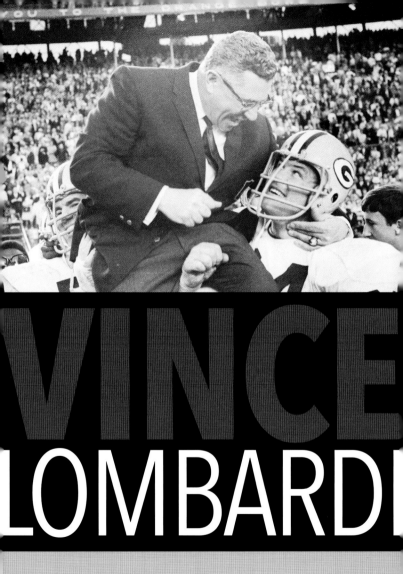

Professional football coach Vince Lombardi became a national symbol of single-minded determination to win. In nine seasons as the head coach of the previously moribund Green Bay Packers, Lombardi led the team to five NFL championships and to victory in the first two Super Bowls.

At Fordham University, Lombardi played guard on the famous line known as the "Seven Blocks of Granite." He studied law at Fordham and had a brief career as a pro league football player before becoming a high school coach in 1939. After serving as an assistant coach in college and in the pros, he was hired as head coach and general manager of the Green Bay Packers in 1959. His Spartan training regimen and personal drive turned the Green Bay Packers from a team accustomed to defeat to the paragon of victory.

He went on to become head coach, general manager, and part owner of the Washington Redskins before dying of cancer in 1970.

Confidence is contagious and
so is lack of confidence.

Leaders are made, they are not born.
They are made by **hard effort,** which
is the price which all of us must pay to
achieve any goal which is worthwhile.

Once you learn to quit, it becomes a habit.

Once you have established the goals you want and the price you're willing to pay, you can ignore the minor hurts, the opponent's pressure, and the temporary failures.

▼

The **price of success** is hard work, dedication to the job, and the determination that, whether we win or lose, we have applied the best of ourselves to the task at hand.

Individual **commitment** to a group effort—that is what makes a team work, a company work, a society work, a civilization work.

▼

Man's finest hour is the moment when he has worked his heart out in a good cause and lies exhausted on the field of battle **victorious.**

The QUALITY of a person's life is in direct proportion to their commitment to excellence, regardless of their chosen field of endeavor.

VINCE LOMBARDI

Mental toughness is many things and rather difficult to explain. Its qualities are sacrifice and self-denial.

▼

The difference between a successful person and others is not a lack of strength, not a lack of knowledge, but rather in a **lack of will.**

Some of us will do our jobs well and some will not, but we will all be judged on one thing: the RESULT.

"

I came through and
I shall return.

"

DOUGLAS
MACARTHUR

Douglas MacArthur graduated from West Point with the highest honors in his class. Brilliant and controversial, he carried his ambition and lust for achievement through posts in World War I, World War II, and the Korean War.

During the course of World War I, MacArthur was promoted to full general and became army chief of staff. MacArthur battled the Japanese in the Philippines during World War II and served as Allied commander of the Japanese occupation.

The Korean War began in 1950, and MacArthur was soon selected to command United Nations forces there. After initial success, he then encountered massive Chinese resistance and entered into a bitter dispute with President Truman. Despite Truman's insistence on a limited war, MacArthur persisted in initiating the offensive. He was relieved of command by Truman for insubordination in 1951. Ever aloof and enigmatic, MacArthur retired to private life, the symbol of zealous dedication to duty, honor, and country.

DOUGLAS MACARTHUR

In war there is no substitute for **victory.**

▼

The history of failure in war can almost

be summed up in two words: too late.

DOUGLAS MACARTHUR

Moral **courage,** the courage of one's convictions, the courage to see things through the eyes of the world—is in a constant conspiracy against the brave. It is the age-old struggle—the roar of the crowd on one side and the voice of your conscience on the other.

**A good head
and a good
heart are always
a formidable
combination.**

NELSON
MANDELA

NELSON MANDELA

Nelson Rolihlahla Mandela was the first president of South Africa to be elected in fully representative democratic elections. He joined the African National Congress, ANC, in 1944 and was an anti-apartheid activist. Mandela was imprisoned for plotting to overthrow the government to end apartheid.

Throughout his twenty-seven years in prison, Nelson Mandela rejected any compromise of his political position to procure his freedom. Upon his release in 1990, Mandela proclaimed his commitment to reconciliation and peace with the country's white minority. During his presidency from 1994 to 1999, he oversaw the transition from minority rule and apartheid.

After retirement, Mandela became an advocate for numerous social and human rights organizations. He was honored with more than a hundred awards in recognition of his tireless dedication and contribution to these causes. Nelson Mandela's strong ideals of international understanding and peace continue to impact the world.

NELSON MANDELA

For to be free is not merely to cast off one's chains, but to live in a way that respects and enhances the FREEDOM of others.

Education is the most powerful weapon
we can use to change the world.

▼

True **reconciliation** does not consist
in merely forgetting the past.

▼

After climbing a great hill, one only finds
that there are many more hills to climb.

The first thing is to be **honest with yourself.** You can never have an impact on society if you have not changed yourself… Great peacemakers are all people of integrity, of honesty, and humility.

▼

The brave man is not he who does not feel afraid, but he who conquers that fear.

Man's goodness is a flame that can be hidden but never extinguished.

▼

We can't afford to stand divided… If we **stand together,** victory of the liberation movement is assured.

NELSON MANDELA

No one is born hating another person because of the color of his skin, or his background, or his religion. People must learn to hate, and if they can learn to hate, they can be taught to **love,** for love comes more naturally to the human heart than its opposite.

There is **no passion to be found playing small**—in settling for a life that is less than the one you are capable of living.

▼

There can be no keener revelation of a society's **soul** than the way in which it treats its children.

Leaders are important but HISTORY is ultimately not made by kings and generals. It is made by the masses.

I have cherished the ideal of a democratic and free society in which all persons will **live together in harmony** and with **equal opportunities.** It is an ideal which I hope to live for and to achieve. But, my lord, if needs be, it is an ideal for which I am prepared to die.

One cannot and must not try to erase the past merely because it does not fit the present.

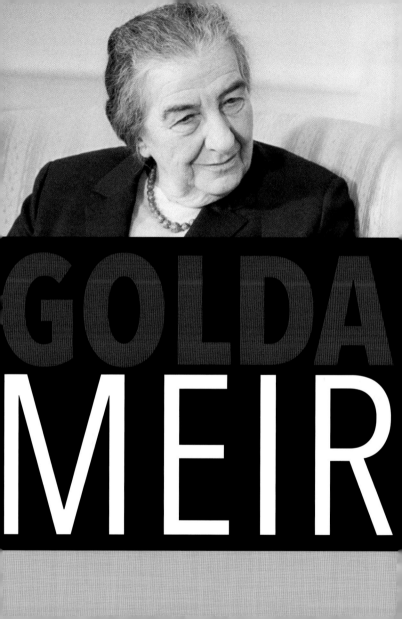

GOLDA
MEIR

GOLDA MEIR

olda Meir was a founder of the State of Israel and served as its fourth prime minister. Born in Kiev, Ukraine, she emigrated to Wisconsin in 1906. Her political activity began as a leader in the Milwaukee Labor Zionist Party.

After emigrating to Palestine in 1921, she held key posts in the Jewish Agency and in the World Zionist

Organization. After Israel proclaimed its independence in 1948, she served as minister of labor and then foreign minister. Meir was elected prime minister in 1969.

During her administration, she worked for a peace settlement in the Middle East using diplomatic means. However, these efforts were interrupted by the outbreak of the fourth Arab-Israeli war. She resigned her post in 1974 but remained an important political figure throughout her retirement.

Golda Meir's true strength and spirit were emphasized when, after her death in 1978, it was revealed that she had suffered from leukemia for twelve years.

GOLDA MEIR

I never did anything ALONE. Whatever was accomplished in this country was accomplished collectively.

I must govern the clock, not
be governed by it.

I have faced **difficult problems** in the
past but nothing like the one I'm faced
with now in leading the country.

Don't be humble. **You aren't that great.**

Old age is like a plane flying through a storm. Once you're aboard, there's **nothing you can do.**

▼

One cannot and must not try to erase the past merely because it does not fit the present.

There's no difference between one's killing and making decisions that will send OTHERS to kill. It's exactly the same thing, or even worse.

Trust yourself. Create the kind of self that you will be happy to live with all of your life. **Make the most of yourself** by fanning the tiny, inner sparks of possibility into flames of achievement.

▼

Those who don't know how to weep with their **whole heart** don't know how to laugh either.

I can honestly say that I was never affected by the question of the success of an undertaking. If I felt it was the **right thing to do,** I was for it regardless of the possible outcome.

"

Success is only
meaningful and
enjoyable if it feels
like your own.

"

MICHELLE
OBAMA

MICHELLE OBAMA

Born in Chicago, Illinois, on a cold day in January 1964, Michelle Obama has gone from sharing a one-bedroom apartment with her parents and older brother to living in the White House as the forty-fourth First Lady of the United States. A graduate of Princeton and Harvard Law, Obama was working at a Chicago law firm when she met her husband and future U.S. President Barack Obama.

Her reign as First Lady has been focused almost entirely on current social issues, specifically poverty, healthy living, and education for women and children. For Obama, it seems no cause is too small—even volunteering in Washington D.C.–area soup kitchens and homeless shelters without pretense. Continually pushing for healthy living, Michelle is a strong supporter of the organic food movement, helping schools plant gardens and putting large efforts into campaigns to end childhood obesity.

You can't make
DECISIONS based on
fear and the possibility
of what might happen.

One of the lessons that I grew up with was to always **stay true to yourself** and never let what somebody else says distract you from your goals. And so when I hear about negative and false attacks, I really don't invest any energy in them, because **I know who I am.**

Every day, the people I meet inspire me... every day, they make me proud...every day they remind me how BLESSED we are to live in the greatest nation on earth.

We learned about dignity and decency—
that how hard you work matters more than
how much you make...that **helping others**
means more than just getting ahead yourself.

I am an example of what is possible when girls from the very beginning of their lives are loved and nurtured by people around them. I was surrounded by **extraordinary women** in my life who taught me about **quiet strength and dignity.**

You may not always have a comfortable life and you will not always be able to solve all of the world's problems at once, but don't ever underestimate the importance you can have because history has shown us that **courage** can be contagious and hope can take on a life of its own.

I wake up every morning in a house that was built by slaves. And I watch my daughters, two beautiful, intelligent, black young women playing with their dogs on the White House lawn… And as my daughters prepare to set out into the world, **I want a leader who is worthy of that truth,** a leader who is worthy of my girls' promise and all our kids' promise, a leader who will be guided every day by the love and hope and impossibly big dreams that we all have for our children.

.

"

Success is how high
you bounce when
you hit bottom.

GEORGE

S. PATTON

Relentless, hard-driving, and tenacious are only a few adjectives to describe George S. Patton Jr., one of the foremost American combat generals of World War II. He was the chief proponent of the adoption of mobile weapons and armored vehicles, and his bravery as a tank commander played a major role in halting the German counterattack at the Battle of the Bulge.

His ruthless sweep across France in the summer of 1944 defied conventional military wisdom but culminated in spectacular success. By January 1945, Patton's forces had reached the German border, capturing thousands of German troops.

GEORGE S. PATTON

Patton was one of the most colorful and controversial figures in military history. Although his outspoken comments and unpredictable actions were often criticized by civilian authorities, he instilled exceptional pride in his men. His toughness earned him the nickname "Old Blood-and-Guts."

By perseverance, study, and eternal desire, any man can become **great.**

▼

If a man does his best, what else is there?

▼

It is only by **doing things** others have not that one can advance.

Moral courage is the most valuable and usually the most absent characteristic in men.

▼

Good tactics can **save** even the worst strategy. Bad tactics will **destroy** even the best strategy.

Lead me, follow me, or **get out of my way.**

▼

Courage is **fear** holding on a minute longer.

▼

An army is a team. It lives, sleeps,

eats, and fights as a team.

GEORGE S. PATTON

A man must know his DESTINY... If he does not recognize it, then he is lost.

" I know in my heart that man is good. That what is right will always eventually triumph. And there is purpose and worth to each and every life.

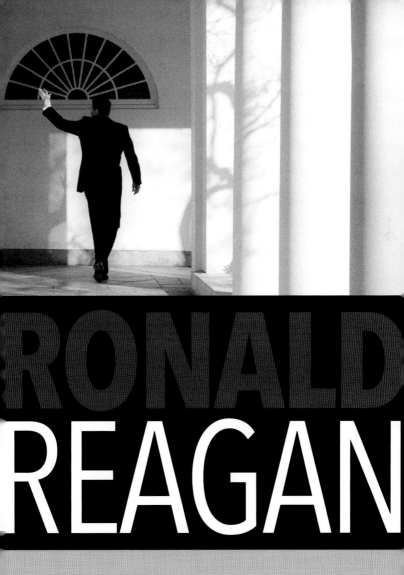

RONALD
REAGAN

The fortieth president of the United States, Ronald Reagan was dubbed "The Great Communicator." He has been credited with restoring optimism to the American people and being instrumental in the 1991 downfall of the Soviet Union. Reagan was known for his ability to convey ideas in a persuasive and well-delivered speaking style. He shifted from an early Democratic Party affiliation and moved into Republican politics. During his presidency, he sustained an adversarial approach to the USSR. Reagan made the abolition of communism and the implementation of supply-side economics the primary focus of his time in office.

Throughout the duration of his term as president, Reagan was committed to the ideologies of democratic capitalism. He departed from office immensely popular, and of Americans polled, 87 percent chose Ronald Reagan as one of the most popular U.S. presidents.

RONALD REAGAN

Freedom is a fragile thing and is never more than one generation away from extinction. It is not ours by inheritance; **it must be fought for and defended constantly by each generation,** for it comes only once to a people. Those who have known freedom and then lost it have never known it again.

You can tell a lot about a fellow's character by his way of eating JELLY BEANS.

There are no easy answers, **but there are simple answers.** We must have the courage to do what we know is morally right.

▼

I don't pay much attention to critics. The world is divided into two kinds of people: those who **can,** and those who **criticize.**

Entrepreneurs and their small enterprises are responsible for almost all the economic growth in the United States.

▼

Freedom is one of the deepest and noblest **aspirations** of the human spirit.

What should happen when you make a mistake is this: you take your knocks, you learn your lessons, and then you move on.

▼

We're too great a nation to limit ourselves to small dreams.

▼

The best minds are not in government. If any were, business would hire them away.

I'm convinced, more than ever, that man finds liberation only when he binds himself to God and commits himself to his fellow man.

▼

Life is one grand, sweet song,

so **start the music.**

They say the world has become too complex for SIMPLE answers. They are wrong.

Our **forbearance** should never be misunderstood. Our **reluctance** for conflict should not be misjudged as failure of will. When action is required to **preserve** our national security, we will act.

"

You must do the
thing you think
you cannot do.

"

ELEANOR
ROOSEVELT

ELEANOR ROOSEVELT

nna Eleanor Roosevelt, known to most simply as Eleanor, was a United Nations diplomat, humanitarian, and wife of President Franklin D. Roosevelt. More than that, though, Eleanor Roosevelt was one of the most widely admired women in the world, and to this day she continues to be an inspiration to many. In particular, she is recognized for her outspoken nature and controversial viewpoints—Roosevelt refused to stand idly by her husband when she saw a need to answer.

During her twelve years as First Lady (1933–1945), the unprecedented breadth of her activities and advocacy of liberal causes made her nearly as controversial a figure as her husband. Roosevelt instituted regular White House press conferences for female correspondents for the first time. In deference to the president's illness, she helped serve as his "eyes and ears" throughout the country. She showed particular interest in such humanitarian concerns as child welfare, slum clearance projects, and equal rights.

After President Roosevelt's death in 1945, President Harry Truman appointed Eleanor Roosevelt a delegate to the United Nations, where, as chair of the UN Commission on Human Rights, she played a major role in the drafting and adoption of the Universal Declaration of Human Rights.

Freedom makes a huge requirement of every human being. With freedom comes **responsibility.** For the person who is unwilling to grow up, the person who does not want to carry his own weight, this is a frightening prospect.

All big changes in human history have been arrived at slowly and through many **compromises.** Happiness is not a goal; it is a byproduct.

▼

Only a man's character is the **real criterion** of worth.

It isn't enough to talk about peace. One must believe in it. And it isn't enough to believe in it. One must work at it.

▼

Justice cannot be for one side alone, but must be for **both.**

ELEANOR ROOSEVELT

Life was meant to be lived, and curiosity must be **kept alive.** One must never, for whatever reason, turn his back on life.

The **giving of love** is an education in itself.

ELEANOR ROOSEVELT

What one has to do usually can be done.

▼

When you cease to make a
contribution, you begin to die.

You gain strength, courage, and confidence by every experience in which you stop to **look fear in the face...** You must do the thing you think you cannot do.

▼

It is not fair to ask of others what you are not willing to do yourself.

"

To reach a port, we must sail—sail, not tie at anchor—sail, not drift.

FRANKLIN
ROOSEVELT

The thirty-second president of the United States, Franklin Delano Roosevelt served for more than twelve years, longer than any other man. He greatly expanded federal powers to affect economic recovery during the Great Depression and was a major Allied leader during World War II.

Roosevelt attended Harvard University and the Columbia University School of Law. He was elected to the New York Senate in 1910 and became assistant secretary of the navy three years later. He remained active in Democratic politics despite being stricken by polio and was elected governor of New York in 1928.

FRANKLIN ROOSEVELT

Elected president in 1932, Roosevelt quickly obtained passage of a sweeping economic program, the New Deal, which provided relief, loans, and jobs through a variety of federal agencies. Roosevelt mobilized industry for military production and extended aid to Great Britain. He played a leading role in creating the alliance with Britain and the USSR that led to victory in World War II.

FRANKLIN ROOSEVELT

Confidence…thrives on honesty, on honor, on the sacredness of obligations, on faithful protection and on unselfish performance. **Without them it cannot live.**

▼

Human kindness has never weakened the stamina or softened the fiber of a free people. A nation does not have to be cruel to be tough.

Happiness lies not in the mere possession of money; it lies in the **joy of achievement,** in the thrill of creative effort.

▼

I'm not the smartest fellow in the world, but I can sure pick smart colleagues.

If civilization is to survive, we must **cultivate the science of human relationships**—the ability of all peoples, of all kinds, to live together and work together, in the same world, at peace.

In our seeking for economic and political progress as a nation, we all go up, or else we all go down, as one people.

Rules are not necessarily sacred; PRINCIPLES are.

Men are not prisoners of fate, but only prisoners of their own minds.

▼

Physical strength can never permanently withstand the impact of spiritual force.

▼

The only limit to our realization of tomorrow will be our doubts of today.

FRANKLIN ROOSEVELT

The only thing we have to fear is fear itself.

The work, my friends, is **peace.** More than an end of this war—an end to the beginnings of all wars.

The truth is found when men are free to **pursue it.**

There are many ways of going forward, but only one way of standing still.

▼

The test of our progress is not whether we add more to the abundance of those who have much; **it is whether we provide enough** for those who have too little.

We, and all others who BELIEVE as deeply as we do, would rather die on our feet than live on our knees.

"

Do what you
can, with what
you have, where
you are.

THEODORE
ROOSEVELT

THEODORE ROOSEVELT

Soldier, statesman, writer, and explorer, Theodore Roosevelt became the twenty-sixth president of the United States. His enormous energy and zest for life made him one of America's most flamboyant leaders.

Roosevelt served as assistant secretary of the navy before resigning in 1898 to fight in the Spanish-American War. Returning as something of a war hero, he was easily elected governor of New York. He then served as vice president of the United States and took office after McKinley's assassination in 1901.

Roosevelt greatly expanded the powers of the presidency and of the federal government on the side of public interest in conflicts between big business and big labor. He won the Nobel Peace Prize in 1906 for mediating the end of the Russo-Japanese War and promoted the construction of the Panama Canal. A devout naturalist, Roosevelt was responsible for setting aside thousands of acres of land to preserve what are today our national parks and forests.

THEODORE ROOSEVELT

I care not what others think of what I do, but I care very much about what I think of what I do! That is character!

▼

Character, in the long run, is the **decisive factor in the life** of an individual and of nations alike.

Far and away the best PRIZE that life has to offer is the chance to work hard at work worth doing.

THEODORE ROOSEVELT

Far better is it to **dare mighty things,** to win glorious triumphs, even though checkered by failure, than to rank with those poor spirits who neither enjoy much nor suffer much, because they live in that gray twilight that knows neither victory nor defeat.

It is hard to fail, but it is worse
never to have tried to succeed.

▼

Great thoughts speak only to the thoughtful
mind, but great actions speak to all mankind.

Keep your eyes on the STARS, but remember to keep your feet on the ground.

THEODORE ROOSEVELT

No man is worth his salt who is not **ready at all times** to risk his well-being, to risk his body, to risk his life, in a great cause.

▼

People ask the difference between a leader and a boss. The leader **leads,** and the boss drives.

Speak softly and carry a big
stick; you will go far.

▼

The best executive is one who has
sense enough to **pick good people
to do what he wants done,** and
self-restraint enough to keep from
meddling with them while they do it.

THEODORE ROOSEVELT

To educate a man in **mind** and not in morals is to educate a menace to society.

▼

The only man who never makes a mistake is the man who never does anything.

There has never yet been a man in our history who led a life of ease whose name is WORTH remembering.

THEODORE ROOSEVELT

The credit belongs to the man who is actually in the arena; whose face is marred by dust and sweat and blood; who strives valiantly; who errs and comes short again and again…**who knows the great enthusiasms,** the great devotions; who spends himself in a worthy cause; who at the best knows in the end the triumph of high achievement; and who at the worst, if he fails, at least fails daring greatly.

"At the very moment when, at sunset, we were making our way through a herd of hippopotamuses, there flashed upon my mind, unforeseen and unsought, the phrase, 'reverence for life.'

ALBERT
SCHWEITZER

ALBERT SCHWEITZER

Albert Schweitzer, who has been called one of the greatest Christians of his time, was a brilliant philosopher, musician, theologian, and physician.

Schweitzer was born in 1875 in Alsace, Germany. At the age of twenty-one, he decided to devote the next nine years of his life to science, music, and preaching. By the time he was thirty, he had an international reputation as a writer on theology, a gifted organist, and an authority on the life and works of Johann Sebastian Bach.

While principal of the Theological College of St. Thomas, he became inspired to become a medical missionary. After studying medicine and surgery for six years, he built his own hospital in Africa. Schweitzer used the proceeds from his concerts and lectures to equip and maintain the hospital. He later set up a leper colony.

Public acknowledgment of his selfless commitment to humanity was bestowed upon him in 1953 when he won the Nobel Peace Prize.

A great **secret of success** is to go through life as a man who never gets used up.

▼

As soon as man does not take his existence for granted, but beholds it as something **unfathomably mysterious,** thought begins.

An optimist is a person who sees a green light everywhere, while the pessimist sees only the red stoplight. The truly WISE person is colorblind.

Constant **kindness** can accomplish much. As the sun makes ice melt, kindness causes misunderstanding, mistrust, and hostility to evaporate.

Example is leadership.

Ethics is nothing else than **reverence for life.**

Do something wonderful;

people may imitate it.

Example is not the main thing in

influencing others. It is the **only** thing.

I don't know what your destiny will be, but one thing I know: the only ones among you who will be really happy are those who will have sought and found how to serve.

▼

The purpose of human life is to **serve** and to show **compassion** and the will to **help** others.

If a man loses his reverence for any part of life, he will lose his reverence for all of life.

▼

Life becomes **harder** for us when we live for others, but it also becomes **richer** and **happier.**

One who gains strength by overcoming obstacles possesses the only strength which can **overcome adversity.**

I can do no other than be reverent before everything that is called life. I can do no other than to have compassion for all that is called life. That is the beginning and the foundation of all ethics.

Truth has no special time of its own. Its hour is NOW—always, and indeed then most truly when it seems most unsuitable to actual circumstances.

" I have a woman's ability to stick to a job and get on with it when everyone else walks off and leaves it. "

MARGARET
THATCHER

Margaret Thatcher was the first woman in European history to be elected prime minister.

The daughter of a grocer, she received her degree in chemistry at Oxford, where she became president of the University Conservative Association. During the 1950s, she worked as a research chemist and also studied law, specializing in taxation.

Thatcher ran for Parliament in 1950, but it was not until 1959 that she was finally elected to the House of Commons. She served as parliamentary secretary to the Ministry of Pensions and National Insurance, and later as education minister. She was elected the leader of the Conservative Party in 1975, and the party's victory in the 1979 elections elevated her to the office of prime minister.

Margaret Thatcher became known as the "Iron Lady" because of her dedication to the ideals in which she believed and the grace to get them accomplished.

What is success? I think it is a mixture of having a flair for the thing that you are doing; knowing that it is not enough, that you have got to have hard work and a certain sense of **purpose.**

Europe was created by history. America was created by philosophy.

▼

I am extraordinarily **patient,** provided I get my own way in the end.

Pennies don't fall from heaven. They have to be **earned** on earth.

▼

I love argument, I love debate. I don't expect anyone just to sit there and agree with me, that's not their job.

Let our CHILDREN grow tall, and some taller than others if they have it in them to do so.

“

I never gave anybody hell. I just told the truth, and they thought it was hell.

HARRY S. TRUMAN

The thirty-third president of the United States, Harry S. Truman faced the tumultuous years at the close of World War II with the blend of honesty, grit, and determination that would make him a modern folk hero.

After serving as a captain in World War I, he became a judge and senator before becoming vice president. When Franklin D. Roosevelt died in 1945,

Truman was suddenly faced with some of the most difficult decisions in U.S. history. In swift order, he made final arrangements for the charter-writing meeting of the United Nations, helped arrange Germany's unconditional surrender, attended a summit meeting at

Potsdam, and brought an end to the war in the Pacific by using the atomic bomb on Hiroshima and Nagasaki.

Elected in his own right in 1948, he went on to implement the Marshall Plan for economic recovery in Western Europe and to form the North Atlantic Treaty Organization (NATO) pact, a collective security agreement with non-Communist European nations.

A president needs political understanding to **run** the government, but he may be **elected** without it.

▼

Whenever you have an efficient government, you have a dictatorship.

America was not built on fear. America was built on **courage, on imagination, and an unbeatable determination** to do the job at hand.

I would rather have PEACE in the world than be president.

It is understanding that gives us an ability to have peace. When we understand the other fellow's **viewpoint,** and he understands ours, then we can sit down and **work out** our differences.

"

Individuals don't win. Teams do.

"

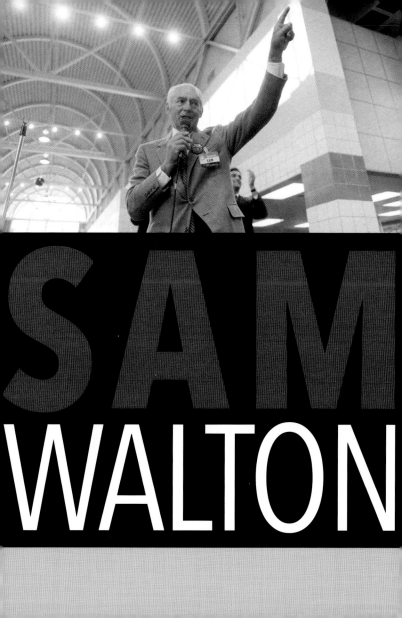

SAM
WALTON

A child of the Depression, Sam Walton came from humble and hard-working roots. As a pioneering retailer, he made the discount-shopping store a phenomenal success in America.

Walton began his retail career in 1940. He and his brother opened the first Wal-Mart discount store in 1962 in Arkansas.

Cutting costs to the absolute minimum and passing the savings on to the customer, along with advanced computerization and automated distribution centers, became the keys to the success of Wal-Mart.

Stores opened across the country, and Wal-Mart became the world's largest retailer in 1991.

Today, Sam Walton's empire has grown to over 3,000 stores with sales over $134 billion. His enterprising and innovative dream continues to grow.

High expectations are the **key** to everything.

▼

Outstanding leaders go out of their way to
boost the self-esteem of their personnel.
If people believe in themselves, it's
amazing what they can accomplish.

I have always been driven to buck the system, to innovate, to **take things beyond where they've been.**

▼

We let folks know we're interested in them and that they're **vital** to us, 'cause they are.

There is only ONE boss.
The customer. And he
can fire everybody in
the company from the
chairman on down,
simply by spending his
money somewhere else.

Appreciate everything your associates do for the business. Nothing else can quite substitute for a few well-chosen, well-timed, **sincere words of praise.** They're absolutely free and worth a fortune.

"

There are two ways of exerting one's strength: one is pushing down, the other is pulling up.

"

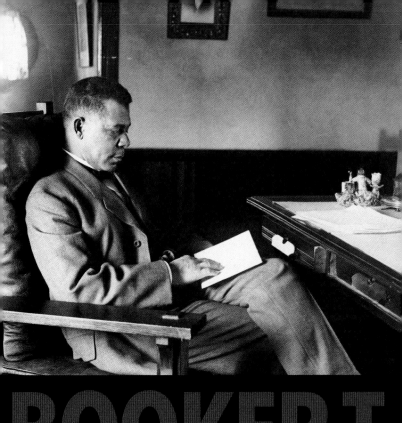

BOOKER T.
WASHINGTON

Born into slavery in 1856, Booker T. Washington went on to become the most influential black leader and educator of his time. He believed that blacks could benefit more from a practical, vocational education than a college education. His work toward economic prosperity for blacks led to his role as founder and head of Tuskegee Institute, a vocational school for blacks in Tuskegee, Alabama.

The success of Tuskegee Institute as well as Washington's strong belief in mutual progress of blacks and whites made him a shrewd political leader and an advisor to presidents, congressmen, and governors. His autobiography *Up from Slavery* was a bestseller that described his rise to national prominence.

In a period of escalating racial tension, Washington's supportive approach was popular with most blacks and whites alike. This period became justly known as the "Age of Booker T. Washington."

Character is **power.**

▼

Nothing ever comes to one, that is worth

having, except as a result of **hard work.**

BOOKER T. WASHINGTON

Few things can help an
individual more than to
place responsibility on
him, and to let him know
that you TRUST him.

CHARACTER, not circumstances, makes the man.

I have learned that success is to be measured not so much by the position that one has reached in life as by the obstacles which he has **overcome while trying to succeed.**

BOOKER T. WASHINGTON

One man cannot hold another man

down in the ditch without remaining

down in the ditch with him.

We must reinforce argument with **results.**

▼

There is no power on earth that can **neutralize the influence** of a high, pure, simple, and useful life.

"

Labor to keep alive
in your breast
that little spark of
celestial fire called
conscience.

"

GEORGE
WASHINGTON

American general, commander in chief of the colonial armies in the American Revolution, and subsequently the first president of the United States, George Washington became known as the father of his country.

Born into a wealthy family of Virginia planters, Washington worked as a surveyor and gained military

experience in the French and Indian War. The impending American Revolution would call him to his country's aid.

Washington was named commander in chief of the military force of all the colonies in 1775. Over the next five years, including the nadir of the harsh winter at Valley Forge, Washington held the American forces together by sheer strength of character. His capture of Cornwallis at Yorktown in 1781 marked the end of the war.

Alone commanding the respect of both parties, Washington was chosen unanimously to preside over the Constitutional Convention. He was elected the country's first president in 1789 and reelected four years later.

GEORGE WASHINGTON

A slender acquaintance with the world must convince every man that *actions*, not words, are the true criterion of the attachment of his friends.

▼

Be **courteous** to all, but intimate with few, and let those few be well tried before you give them **your confidence.**

Few men have virtue to withstand the highest bidder.

▼

Human **happiness** and moral **duty** are inseparably connected.

▼

If the freedom of speech is taken away then dumb and silent we may be led, like sheep to the slaughter.

Let your heart feel
for the afflictions and
distress of everyone, and
let your HAND give in
proportion to your purse.

GEORGE WASHINGTON

True friendship is a plant of slow growth,
and must undergo and withstand
the shocks of adversity before it
is entitled to the appellation.

I hope I shall possess firmness and
virtue enough to maintain what I
consider the most enviable of all titles,
the character of an **honest** man.

Liberty, when it begins to take root,
is a plant of rapid growth.

▼

It is better to offer **no excuse** than a bad one.

▼

Our cruel and unrelenting enemy leaves
us only the choice of brave resistance,
or the most abject submission. We have,
therefore, to resolve to conquer or die.

Truth will ultimately PREVAIL where there are pains taken to bring it to light.

" "

Failure is not fatal
but failure to change
might be.

JOHN
WOODEN

A keen student of the game and a master motivator, John Wooden was one of the greatest coaches in college basketball history. He led his teams at the University of California at Los Angeles to a record ten NCAA championships.

As a player at Purdue University, Wooden earned All-America honors in 1930, 1931, and 1932. He coached high school basketball before serving in the U.S. Navy during World War II. After the war, he became head basketball coach and athletic director

JOHN WOODEN

at Indiana State Teachers College. He was appointed head coach at UCLA in 1948.

Adversity is the state in which man most easily becomes acquainted with himself.

▼

Be prepared and be **honest.**

Be more concerned with your **character** than your reputation, because your character is what you really are, while your reputation is merely what others think you are.

▼

Consider the rights of others before your own feelings, and the feelings of others before your own rights.

JOHN WOODEN

Do not let what you cannot do interfere with **what you can do.**

Never mistake activity for achievement.

You can't live a perfect day without doing **something for someone** who will never be able to repay you.

▼

Don't measure yourself by what you have accomplished, but by what you should have accomplished with your ability.

"

The future
starts today, not
tomorrow.

POPE
JOHN PAUL II

When Pope John Paul II was invested in 1978, he became the first Polish pope in the Church's history—and the first non-Italian pope in 456 years. This remarkable man encompassed the globe to bring the doctrine of the Catholic Church to the world's people.

Born Karol Wojtyla in Wadowice, Poland, he studied Polish literature and worked in a chemical factory before the outbreak of World War II. Determined to become a priest, he went into hiding at the palace of the archbishop of Krakow and was ordained in 1946. He later became archbishop of Krakow after receiving a doctorate in ethics and becoming a professor of philosophy. He was made cardinal in 1967 and elected pope just over ten years later.

His fluency in a number of languages uniquely qualified him as an international ambassador for the Church. His passionate commitment to spread the word of God continued until his death in 2005.

How can we profess faith in God's word, and then refuse to let it inspire and direct our thinking, our activity, our decisions, and our responsibilities toward one another?

▼

Peace is not just the absence of war… Like a cathedral, peace must be **constructed patiently** and with unshakable faith.

POPE JOHN PAUL II

The **truth** is not always the same
as the majority decision.

▼

The worst prison would be a closed heart.

▼

Love is never defeated.

Let us not accept violence as the way of peace. Let us instead **begin by respecting true freedom:** the resulting peace will be able to satisfy the world's expectations, for it will be a peace built on justice, a peace founded on the incomparable dignity of the free human being.

Freedom consists not in doing what we like, but in having the right to do what we OUGHT.

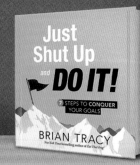
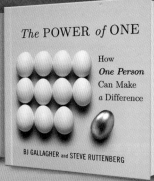